T0167454

RAND

School Decentralization

Lessons from the Study of Bureaucracy

Bruce Bimber

Supported by the
George Gund Foundation
and the Lilly Endowment Inc.

**Institute on
Education and Training**

RAND's Institute on Education and Training conducts policy analysis to help improve education and training for all Americans.

The Institute examines *all* forms of education and training that people may get during their lives. These include formal schooling from preschool through college; employer-provided training (civilian and military); post-graduate education; proprietary trade schools; and the informal learning that occurs in families, in communities, and with exposure to the media. Reexamining the field's most basic premises, the Institute goes beyond the narrow concerns of each component to view the education and training enterprise as a whole. It pays special attention to how the parts of the enterprise affect one another and how they are shaped by the larger environment. The Institute:

- examines the performance of the education and training system

- analyzes problems and issues raised by economic, demographic, and national security trends

- evaluates the impact of policies on broad, system-wide concerns

- helps decisionmakers formulate and implement effective solutions.

To ensure that its research affects policy and practice, the Institute conducts outreach and disseminates findings to policymakers, educators, researchers, and the public. It also trains policy analysts in the field of education.

RAND is a private, nonprofit institution, incorporated in 1948, which engages in nonpartisan research and analysis on problems of national security and the public welfare. The Institute builds on RAND's long tradition—interdisciplinary, empirical research held to the highest standards of quality, objectivity, and independence.

This report focuses on decentralization, an idea that is thought to be a key to improving productivity in education and the private sector, and seeks to answer the following questions:

- What does the term *decentralization* mean, and how do its advocates think it can improve public-school performance?

- What management arrangements are implied by decentralization, and how will those arrangements affect the people who work in schools and those who would hold teachers and principals accountable for performance?

Preliminary answers to these questions are proposed and are based on social science theory, and business and public-sector experience. The ideas presented here will be incorporated in a forthcoming Institute on Education and Training (IET) report on alternative governance systems for public education.

Researchers concerned with the theoretical underpinnings of proposals for education reform are the main audience of this report. The report should also provide fresh insights for school superintendents, board members, teachers' union heads, and civic leaders concerned with improving the performance of public-school systems.

This report has been funded by the George Gund Foundation and is the first product of the study of governance alternatives for public education sponsored by RAND's Institute on Education and Training with funds from a grant by the Lilly Endowment Inc. The Institute on

Education and Training conducts policy analysis to help improve education and training for all Americans.

CONTENTS

FIGURE

Decentralization has become an organizing principle for much of the education-reform movement in the United States. The concept that less bureaucratic, hierarchical administration of schools will have salutary effects on public education is a common thread running through site-based management efforts, the school choice movement, the drive for teacher professionalization, "effective schools" theories, and attempts to establish independent, for-profit schools. It has almost become an article of faith that greater freedom from the effects of centralized bureaucracy, hierarchy, and administrative rules will serve the interest of improving U.S. schools.

School reform through decentralization is plagued by one important problem: Education reformers disagree fundamentally over what decentralization really entails. For some, *decentralization* means making principals the new locus of authority in schools; for others, it means allowing teachers to play the dominant role in managing the school; and for still others, decentralization points chiefly to increased parent and community participation or to nothing more than reductions in the size of administrative staffs. People speak of decentralization in terms of a panoply of concepts: creating smaller organizational units, reducing hierarchy and red tape, creating shared decisionmaking, and increasing local autonomy.

This report reduces many of these ideas to a common core, with the aim of providing a clear definition of *decentralization* that can guide the restructuring of schools. It examines decentralization within the context of the following four fundamental questions about the reform of school governance. In doing so, it applies lessons from theories about bureaucracy, public administration, and organizations. The answers to these questions are intended for school superintendents, board members, teachers' union heads, civic leaders, and researchers concerned with the reorganization of schools.

What is the fundamental idea behind decentralization?

Decisionmaking authority is the crux of decentralization. *To decentralize* is to shift authority for the making of decisions downward, from the center, or top levels, of a hierarchy toward the local, or bottom, levels. Most of the ideas that are associated with decentralizing, such as cutting levels from a hierarchy, creating initiative, and increasing control by workers, can be reduced to the problem of determining who has authority to make what decisions. Thinking about school governance as a process by which decisions are made about personnel, instruction, budgets, and administration provides a concrete framework for understanding and planning decentralization.

Does decentralization necessarily imply group-decisionmaking arrangements such as parent-teacher committees and "shared decisionmaking"?

Decentralization in schools is commonly equated with the presence of decisionmaking committees and the formal sharing of power among principals, teachers, and, sometimes, parents. Many people have interpreted decentralization as being a process of inclusion and representation. The literature on bureaucracy does not support this view. In fact, there is little to suggest that decentralization is incompatible with strong or focused leadership, provided that leadership is located at the local level. Although it may seem paradoxical to suggest that a decentralized organization can have within it strong leaders, the study of bureaucracies suggests that this is often the case.

The distinction between a decentralized organization and a centralized, or bureaucratic, organization appears to rest not on the presence or absence of decisive leadership but on the location of that leadership in the administrative hierarchy. School reformers must be careful to distinguish between the need for decentralization per se in the form of greater autonomy, discretion, and problem-solving capacity at the level of the school, and the need for more democratic decisionmaking, in the form of inclusiveness and greater capacity to represent the views and interests of teachers and parents. These are rather different reform objectives and do not necessarily call for the same structural changes.

Should a decentralized organization rely primarily on the judgment, standards, and goodwill of professionals to achieve high levels of performance, or should it rely primarily on formal rewards and sanctions tied to performance to motivate workers?

Personnel systems in schools are receiving ever-increasing criticism for severing appraisals of teacher and principal performance from decisions about pay, advancement, and tenure.   The criticism maintains that schools cannot hire the best people, they cannot reward those who stand out, and it is too difficult to get rid of those who chronically fail to measure up.

Such criticisms are supported by several theories of bureaucracy that suggest that decentralized school systems should not rely on current personnel and incentive systems. Agency theory, for example, argues that, if workers are to be expected to contribute reliably to achieving an organization's goals, meaningful connections should exist between workers' performance and the rewards and sanctions they receive. Incentives may be financial, such as bonuses or increases in regular compensation, or more professional, such as promotion opportunities or evaluation. "Professionalization" of teaching is often offered as a solution to problems of teacher performance; however, it, too, requires a system of rewards and sanctions to motivate performance.

How can performance be rewarded without encouraging the return of a focus on compliance and rule-following, the heart of bureaucracy?

Decentralized school designs must find a way to provide incentives and sanctions for employees without falling into the trap of mandating rules specifying what is "proper" behavior or performance, such as how many hours are to be worked each day, how much time is to be spent "on task," or which lessons are to be delivered according to what schedule. Establishing a successful system of incentives requires new ways of assigning responsibility for setting goals, and for devising the means of achieving those goals. This distinction between means and ends is fundamental to the concept of decentralization, although it is rarely discussed explicitly.

One way to implement a division of labor between means and ends is to envision a "contract" between the central office and the school, an agreement that conveys goals and standards set centrally but does not specify how the school is to go about achieving those goals. By contrast, in the rule-based systems of governance, the hallmark of bureaucracy, the main office both sets goals *and* specifies a set of procedures, or rules, intended to be followed to achieve those goals. Consequently, the responsibility of the school is not so much to achieve goals as to follow rules. In a decentralized system of governance, the school is responsible for devising its own procedures and is held accountable on the basis of performance rather than compliance.

ACKNOWLEDGMENTS

This report reflects the comments and suggestions of a number of people at RAND. I am indebted most to Paul Hill for his welcome and thought-provoking reflections on the various drafts and for his enthusiasm about the process of reforming education in the United States. Brian Mittman provided a useful review, and Thomas Glennan, Susan Bodilly, and Michael Mack offered helpful comments along the way. I am also indebted to the teachers, principals, and central-office administrators who have shared their time, concerns, and ideas with me.

Chapter One

INTRODUCTION

Decentralization has become an organizing principle for much of the education-reform movement in the United States. The idea that removing the administration of schools from a central bureaucracy will have salutary effects underlies site-based management efforts, the school choice movement, the drive for teacher professionalization, "effective schools" theories, and attempts to establish independent, for-profit schools. All these movements aim to increase initiative, responsibility, and the capacity of schools to solve problems. It has almost become an article of faith that greater freedom from the effects of centralized bureaucracy, hierarchy, and administrative rules will serve the interest of improving U.S. schools.

The widespread enthusiasm for decentralization masks a fundamental problem: Education reformers disagree over exactly what the concept means. People speak of decentralization in terms of diverse activities, such as creating smaller organizational units, streamlining central-office staffs, reducing hierarchy and red tape, increasing accountability, establishing "local control," and creating "shared decisionmaking." Some decentralization plans make principals the new locus of authority in schools; others rely on teachers to play the dominant role in managing the decentralized school; and still others focus on parent and community participation. Some decentralization plans aim to improve schools simply by cutting the size of administrative staffs. It often appears as though no two school systems agree on what decentralization is or on what roles should be played by teachers, unions, parents, community organizations, principals, school boards, superintendents, and central offices in a "decentralized" school system.

1

FOCUS OF REPORT

This report discusses the main ideas associated with organizational decentralization. The goal of this inquiry is to fill some of the conceptual gaps that exist in our understanding of educational decentralization, using information from the study of other institutions. Guided by the observation that school systems are bureaucracies, and that schools suffer many of the same problems that afflict other bureaucratic organizations, this report applies lessons from theories about bureaucracy to the debate over school reform, examining several fundamental questions about what decentralization involves. The result is a set of organizational principles intended to clarify the ideas underlying the many concepts that are commonly associated with decentralization, organizational principles that can guide the restructuring of schools. These principles come from literature on public administration, organizations, and bureaucracy, and draw on the work of sociologists, political scientists, and economists.

The resulting definition of decentralization should be useful to those persons involved in restructuring schools and who desire decentralization but are faced with a number of sometimes poorly defined or conflicting visions of what form a decentralized school should take. Since much of the experimentation and leadership in school reform is taking place at local levels, the audience for this report includes teachers, principals, administrators, and other educators who seek guidance about the redesign of school-governance arrangements.

Decentralization as a means for overcoming problems of poor performance, lack of initiative, and red tape in government agencies is not a new idea. Since German sociologist Max Weber argued 75 years ago that specialized, hierarchical bureaucracies were the most efficient and effective form of administrative organization, people have debated the merits of centralized and decentralized institutions. Education specialists often tend to treat schools as unique organizations with very special administrative problems, because schools' education and socialization functions lend them a distinctive character among organizations, and because the practice of teaching is thought to generate unique administrative requirements. But these distinctions are not always helpful for thinking about decentralization and the redesign of governance systems. Many of the difficulties that plague U.S. schools are typical of public bureaucracies: a focus on rules and compliance with procedure rather than outcomes; inertia; lack of initiative; and unresponsiveness to changing external needs.

Like other bureaucracies, public-school systems are funded with tax dollars, and they provide a public good that we expect the government to offer but whose precise definition is often a source of disagreement. As with other bureaucracies, we hold schools publicly accountable by electing officials to represent diverse interests, making the education system inherently political, as are all public bureaucracies. Perhaps most important for this comparison, schools are managed through a hierarchical system of administration encumbered with rules and procedures intended to guarantee fairness and equity.

A number of scholars have observed the similarities between schools and other bureaucracies. Schools have been described as "street-level" bureaucracies, like police departments, welfare agencies, and local courts.[1] They have been compared with armies, prisons, and motor-vehicle departments.[2] In *Reinventing Government*, David Osborne and Ted Gaebler include the problems in U.S. schools among the larger category of bureaucratic troubles plaguing almost all public organizations.[3] Using different terms, sociological theory sometimes views schools as "natural systems,"[4] a class of organizations that survive by adapting themselves structurally and procedurally to their political or social environments, rather than by producing a product for distribution. Such adaptation would orient them much more toward rule compliance than toward outcomes and results. Such characteristics make the problems of decentralizing school systems very much like those of decentralizing other government bureaucracies.

---

[1]Lipsky, Michael, *Street Level Bureaucracy,* New York: Russell Sage Foundation, 1980.

[2]Wilson, James Q., *Bureaucracy: What Government Agencies Do and Why They Do It,* New York: Basic Books, 1989.

[3]Osborne, David, and Ted Gaebler, *Reinventing Government: How the Entrepreneurial Spirit Is Transforming the Public Sector,* New York: Addison-Wesley, 1992.

[4]Scott, W. Richard, *Organizations: Rational, Natural, and Open Systems,* 3rd ed., New York: Prentice-Hall, 1992.

DECENTRALIZATION: FOUR QUESTIONS

Four primary questions are emerging in the debate over school decentralization. They concern the basic definition of *decentralization*, the division of responsibility and authority among members of a decentralized school system, and the establishment of new systems of rewards and accountability for schools. The questions are

1. **What is the fundamental idea behind *decentralization*?** No two people speak of decentralization in the same way. Do the many ideas that are commonly associated with decentralization—the search for less paperwork, fewer clearances and approvals, and more autonomy—have a common denominator?

2. **Does decentralization necessarily imply group-decisionmaking arrangements such as parent-teacher committees and "shared decisionmaking"?** The common aim of decentralization is to give more autonomy to schools by devolving authority from the center—the main office, the superintendent, and the board—to the school itself. But once that authority is passed down, questions are raised on how decisions are to be made within the walls of the school; whether decisionmaking should be a shared responsibility, through formal power sharing, or should reside with a strong leader within the school; and what the respective responsibilities of teachers, principals, and parents are in a decentralized system.

3. **Should a decentralized organization rely primarily on the judgment, standards, and goodwill of professionals to achieve high levels of performance, or should it rely primarily on formal rewards and sanctions tied to performance to motivate workers?** Current school personnel systems largely sever pay, promotion, and tenure from appraisals of teacher performance, if appraisals are made at all. Schools should ask whether these systems are useful in a decentralized structure; whether decentralized schools should adopt the labor contracts and civil-service arrangements found in today's more centralized schools, rely on increased teacher professionalization, or establish new systems.

4. **How can performance be rewarded without encouraging the return of a focus on compliance and rule-following?** The heart of what makes bureaucracies so "bureaucratic" is a focus on compliance with rules in the place of an emphasis on results. At issue is how a decentralized school system can assess and reward performance without returning to rule-based evaluations and judgments about compliance.

These interrelated questions underlie much of the debate over school decentralization, and they raise problems that are common to many kinds of institutions. Theories of bureaucracy from several disciplines can suggest some preliminary answers. The next four chapters seek answers, from those theories, to each of the four questions in turn. The final chapter capsulizes those answers as they relate specifically to schools.

Chapter Two

DECENTRALIZATION DEFINED

Decisionmaking authority is the crux of decentralization. *To decentralize* is to shift authority for the making of decisions downward from the topmost levels, or center, of a hierarchy toward the bottom, or local, levels. Most ideas associated with decentralizing, such as streamlining hierarchy, creating initiative, and increasing control by workers, can be reduced to the problem of determining who has authority to make which decisions. The many positive effects people attribute to decentralization, such as less paperwork and fewer clearances, greater local control, and more autonomy, emerge from this core problem. Whether an organization functions in a centralized or decentralized way, and whether it is "bureaucratic" or independent and autonomous, is largely a function of how responsibility for decisions is distributed among various parties.

Thinking about decentralization in this way raises some further definitional questions. Because the operation of complex organizations depends on the making of many decisions by many people located at various places in a hierarchy, decentralization can take place in more than one dimension. In this chapter I define decentralization in terms of those dimensions: the shift of authority down the hierarchy or outside it.

POLITICAL DECENTRALIZATION VERSUS
ADMINISTRATIVE DECENTRALIZATION

Decentralization can take place within an administrative structure or it can involve the shifting of authority outside, to panels or committees. Decentralization that entails changes within an organization's hierarchy can be called "administrative." In this form, decentralization means shifting authority downward *within* the structure of the school system; for example, a central school board yields authority over the hiring of teachers to district superintendents across a large city. As a result, schools have more discretion and the main office has less. Administrative decentralization might also mean that the superintendent gives more authority to schools to make curriculum changes, with teachers and principals gaining the discretion yielded by the district office.

Decentralization that shifts authority *out* of the administrative structure of the school system into the hands of a governing body—a local school board or citizen council—can be called "political." In this form, decentralization devolves power to a lower political body rather than to a lower administrative unit. For example, in 1989, Chicago undertook a form of political decentralization by creating 540 new school councils and giving them authority to participate in decisionmaking. In doing so, the city took power previously wielded in the administrative bureaucracy and gave it to elected bodies outside the existing school structure. The key to political decentralization is that the new locus of power is an outside, politically constituted body rather than an inside administrator or manager who is simply lower in the chain of command.

The distinction between political and administrative decentralization is not always a sharp one. A decentralization plan may well attempt to achieve both forms at once, as did New York City's 1969 School Decentralization Act. That act created the city's Community School Boards, which are composed of elected members, and it gave them certain powers over superintendent selection, curriculum, and teacher hiring. This political decentralization scheme was in many ways at the heart of the reform; however, the law also redistributed administrative authority within the formal hierarchy.

Such dual redistribution also occurs in some site-based management schemes that use a "community control" model for school reform. Administrative decentralization is employed to give teachers more discretion, and political decentralization is implemented to give parents and citizens a say in school governance. Conversely, administrative decentralization plans may sometimes explicitly exclude political decentralization, as in certain site-based management arrangements that give more administrative power to teachers and principals without introducing new sources of political power, such as parent councils.

I draw these distinctions between political and administrative decentralization because their implications and requirements, and the obstacles they are likely to encounter, differ greatly. Political decentralization and administrative decentralization are quite different entities. Consequently, those organizations and individuals planning decentralization must be careful to relate their goals for decentralization to their choice of methods.

LEVELS OF HIERARCHY

Both administrative and political decentralization involve a downward shifting of authority. But because organizations typically have many layers of hierarchy, decentralization can take place among different levels—a fact that can be the source of disagreement among members of an organization about what decentralization means.

Defining decentralization in a hierarchy with many levels, such as a school system, requires clarity about which level is losing power and which is gaining it, as well as which levels may remain unaffected. Decentralizing authority from the top managers to middle-level administrators in an organization may have virtually no effect on the discretion given to line managers at the bottom of the organization. But decentralizing authority from the middle to the bottom may directly affect how employees and first-line managers do their jobs. In the organization depicted in Figure 1, decentralization may mean shifting authority from level A to level B while leaving lower levels unaffected, or it may involve shifts of authority between levels B and C or between C and D. One level's decentralization may be another's status quo.

Even one person's perception of a "decentralized" organization may change over time. The U.S. Congress provides a good example of how perspectives on decentralization can change. In the first decade of this century, the House of Representatives underwent what political scientists call the "Revolution of 1910." Insurgent legislators

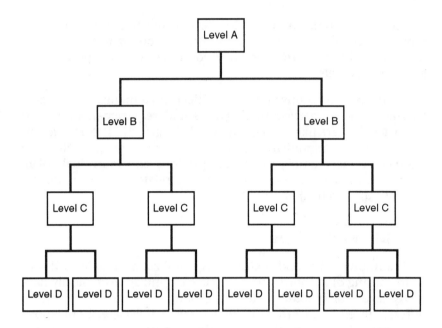

Figure 1—Levels of Hierarchy

"deposed" Speaker of the House Joseph Cannon of Illinois. Cannon had developed what some considered dictatorial powers over the running of the House; he was referred to as "Czar Cannon." A tremendous amount of political power was centralized in Cannon's hands, and insurgent members of both parties sought to shift some of that power downward in the House hierarchy. The result was a decentralized organization in which the committees, party leaders, and, for a while, the Democratic party caucus, gained power at the expense of the speaker.

A half-century later, members of the House staged another form of revolt, this time because they perceived that too much power was "centralized" in the hands of committee leaders or chairs, who had come to be called "barons"—the former recipients of "decentralized" authority. Congress restructured itself in the 1970s, in part in order to decentralize authority from the committee chairs to sub-committees and members not in the leadership hierarchy. The result was an even more decentralized system that many now claim is too fragmented and too parochial to work effectively.

So, whereas in 1910 decentralization meant taking power away from the "Czar" and giving it to the "barons," in the 1970s decentralization meant taking power from the "barons" and giving it to the "gentry." Decentralization can have different meanings at different times, depending on the particular organizational levels of interest.

In the debate over school reform, most would agree that we should be concerned with giving authority to the schools—meaning teachers and principals—rather than shifting authority around within the bureaucracy above the level of the school. But teachers may interpret decentralization to mean that they are to receive more authority and principals, less. At the same time, principals may understand decentralization as something that gives them more control. The issue of control as part of decentralization is the topic of Chapter Three.

LEADERSHIP AND MANAGEMENT UNDER DECENTRALIZATION

One of the main issues for a school in a system that has been decentralized is control of decisionmaking: Who is to manage a school in a decentralized system? If current school-governance arrangements are scrapped, arrangements in which many decisions are made by central-office administrators or school boards, or are regulated and specified by law or contract, choices must be made about whether new authority vested in the individual school should be given to a committee or to a single person. At issue is whether decentralization necessarily entails "democratic" decisionmaking and the formal sharing of power within each school among teachers, parents, and the principal, as is often thought, or decisionmaking by a principal or single manager.

The answer requires that a distinction be made between the function of representation, of bringing forward the interests and expertise of teachers and parents to decisionmakers, and the function of administration, of making decisions about those interests and the operation of the school. Clarifying the purposes of decentralization may involve choosing between these functions.

The literature on bureaucracy does not support the view that decentralization must entail the diffusion of power among workers or the combining of arrangements for representation and administration in local units. In fact, there is little to suggest that decentralization is incompatible with strong or focused leadership being exercised at local levels, rather than in a central office. Instead of requiring that a school devise ways to share power among many people or establish committees to serve leadership functions, a decentralized school system may employ strong principals whose authority is increased by decentralization of authority from the main office. While it may seem paradoxical to suggest that a decentralized organization can have within it strong leaders, the study of bureaucracies suggests that this is often the case.

The distinction between a decentralized organization and a centralized, or *bureaucratic*, organization does not rest on the presence or absence of decisive leaders, but on where decisions are made in the administrative hierarchy. Decentralization weakens centralized control at the top of an organization, distributing authority among local units, but it does not necessarily mean that local units themselves are without strong leadership. On the contrary, decentralization strengthens the hand of local leaders. Whether the organization is a branch office for IBM's sales force, a district office of the U.S. Forest Service, a retail franchise, or a Social Security office, decentralization means only that discretion over decisions rests with managers or leaders who are present where the tasks are being performed.

In the debate over school reform, decentralization is often portrayed in ways that weaken the authority of not only central offices but also principals, by sharing power among teachers and parents. Whatever the merits of such arrangements, such as better representation of teachers' interests, theories of bureaucracy do not support the view that decentralization must entail the weakening of authority at all managerial levels. Often, those who study successful organizations find effective leaders at the local level who direct the efforts of workers and who take responsibility for the success or failure of the organization.[1]

An army provides a good example. Successful armies are often seen as the creation of good generals who exercise strong leadership from the very top. But some military functions are better performed by decentralized units for which leadership and control are located closer to the field, by captains or lieutenants, for example. Commando teams, rescue squads, and other special forces organiza-

---

[1]For a review, see Wilson (1989).

tions must be able to adapt quickly to rapidly changing circumstances and to make judgments and decisions themselves about how to use resources, without consulting supervisors. To have a complex burden of rules, regulations, and clearances would defeat the purpose of such special units.

This does not mean that such units are without decisive leadership, or that they make decisions by voting among members. Instead, some of the traditional authority of the distant commander is delegated to local leaders, who may have great power to command the actions of their units. Special units are far from being leaderless or giving total authority to soldiers themselves. In each decentralized unit, extra power and discretion are given to the leader who is close to the tasks that soldiers are performing. Hence, what might appear to be a paradox develops: From the perspective of the soldier, the immediate leader has more authority under decentralized arrangements than in a traditional hierarchy.

This kind of leadership can serve a local organization in two complementary ways: greater decisiveness and enhanced accountability. Strong local management is likely to lead to more decisiveness than can be achieved through participatory schemes and the absence of professional management. Discussion, voting, and the reaching of group consensus are more cumbersome and prone to internal tension and division than is managerial decisionmaking. Strong leadership can also enhance accountability, since a single leader can more easily be held responsible for an organization's performance than can a committee or panel of decisionmakers, each of whom can represent a different constituency and none of whom shoulders all the responsibility for a given decision. In the army unit, the local leader receives credit for successes, and can ultimately be replaced for failures.

By contrast, in discussions of site-based management, decentralization and increased participation are often confounded. Decentralization in schools is commonly equated with shared decisionmaking, collegial or cooperative control, temporary rotating principalships, and other schemes that diffuse authority over decisions. Consequently, site-based management often takes the form of political decentralization, involving parents and citizens in the making of decisions, or it becomes a form of administrative decentralization in which the new locus of authority is a panel of decisionmakers from within the organization. Both approaches merge the function of administration with the function of representation, minimizing the role for a professional manager or leader, and emphasizing representation of teacher and community interests.

Capable local leaders often play a vital role in the success of decentralization efforts. For this reason, school systems should give careful consideration to setting up power-sharing arrangements as a means for decentralizing. Where the goal of reform is purely decentralization and the reduction of bureaucracy, authority should not necessarily be distributed as widely as possible because decisions are often better made by a professional leader than by committee. The proximate goal of achieving greater school autonomy from the administrative hierarchy does not require that teachers assume responsibility for school management. Leadership authority located in the hands of one person need not be dictatorial or unresponsive to the expertise of teachers. On the continuum of management styles from the "boss" to the administrator who is highly constrained by procedure, successful leaders of decentralized schools can represent a middle ground where leadership is exercised consultatively, but in which responsibility for achieving goals and authority for pursuing them clearly rest with the leader.

Chapter Four

PROFESSIONALISM, REWARDS, AND SANCTIONS

The decision about whether a decentralized school is to be run by teachers, by principals, by parents and teachers, or by some other combination often raises the most contention in the decentralization process. This decision is shaped by the strained and mistrustful relationships that exist between teachers and administrators in many school districts. Some administrators' complaints about present systems of school decisionmaking—that it is too difficult to choose and reward the best teachers and to get rid of those who are ineffective—are met by the opposite complaint from teachers, who argue that they have little recourse against arbitrary or ineffectual principals.

Many on each side would like a stronger system of accountability and performance incentives for the other, yet each is contractually protected from just such changes. The arguments that are used to rationalize current arrangements focus on the ostensibly special nature of teaching, the necessity to protect collegiality and cooperation from the effects of competition, and the nature of professionalism. The impasse over the issue of individual accountability is a major roadblock in the course to restructuring the administration of schools.

The problem that each side raises—whether workers in schools should face greater incentives for good performance and stronger sanctions, including firing, for poor performance—can be reduced to the following: internal or external motivation and incentives. At issue is whether a school's system of governance—including its labor contracts—should assume voluntary or self-directed efforts to excel and contribute toward organizational success, or, instead, should assume that high performance must be explicitly motivated and rewarded. This issue raises the question of whether decentralization is compatible with current personnel policies and contracts, which largely sever pay, promotion, and tenure from appraisals of performance.

STRUCTURE AND ACTION

This issue is often encountered in economics and sociology and is sometimes referred to as the question of "structure and action." It concerns the extent to which institutional structure is responsible for shaping people's behavior and actions. One view of the performance of an organization is that it is primarily the result of the attitudes, motives, skills, and values that people bring to it independently. In this view, the best way to reform an ailing organization is to reinvigorate the people who work there with, for instance, training and better working conditions. Replacing workers with new employees in whom the habits of the past are not ingrained might even be necessary.

An example of this kind of thought can be found in some people's attitudes toward the U.S. Congress, whose public standing has reached unprecedented lows. In the demand for reform of the national legislature, many blame members of Congress themselves. Several states have passed term limits in order to "throw the bums out." These reformers believe that individuals are to blame for the situation in which Congress finds itself, and they look for change to come from new personnel.

But a more comprehensive view of organizational behavior sees the design of an organization itself as responsible for eliciting good behavior, by providing incentives and coordinating people's efforts. In this view, structure shapes action, and the reform of an organization must not focus only on the training, experience, or affective qualities of workers but must address the performance incentives designed into the organization. This line of thought is manifested in the debate over congressional reform in the form of calls for institutional restructuring: a streamlined committee system, clearer chains of authority and jurisdiction, and tighter controls over campaign finance, money, and the perquisites of office. In this view, unless the basic structure of the institution is changed, little will improve, and even an entirely new, untainted group of representatives and senators would fall into the same behavioral patterns as their predecessors.

Calls for school decentralization represent an acceptance of structural assumptions about school systems, at least in part. Decentralization itself aims to improve schools by first changing their basic design as organizations, rather than only by attempting to change the performance of school employees (e.g., by teacher retraining) within the context of current school structures. But carrying this assumption to its conclusion requires more than giving greater autonomy to schools; it requires rethinking the ways in which workers are rewarded. In this view, it is not enough to give greater discretion to teachers and principals, to pay them well, or to provide training and an attractive working environment. If workers are to contribute to an organization's success over the long run, they should labor within a set of incentives and sanctions directed toward that goal. Restructuring an organization's rules and procedures in order to build in these incentives should be part of the process of decentralization.

AGENCY THEORY

A good way to think about the problem of incentives is from the perspective of "agency theory" in political science and economics. In agency theory, structural incentives are inherent in all hierarchical systems, regardless of the kind of work being performed. The theory assumes that the managers of an organization have objectives that are different from those of workers. Managers bear responsibility for achieving the goals of an organization, such as manufacturing a product or providing a service. Workers, on the other hand, are hired agents who, under the terms of a work contract, perform tasks specified by the manager. Workers are interested in getting the best deal they can for themselves. They want to be paid as much as possible for the least required effort on their part. Similarly, managers want to pay as little as possible for the most possible work. According to this scheme, workers' interests are intrinsically at odds with those of their employers.

An inherent feature of this relationship is that agents benefit from an "information asymmetry": Workers have more information than do managers about, for example, how the work is being performed, what is being accomplished, how hard they are working, and how much they are contributing toward the organization's goals. For managers to acquire this information is usually very difficult and expensive in terms of oversight and supervision, so workers have more information about how the work contract is being fulfilled than do managers.

In agency theory,[1] employees can exploit the lack of information on the part of managers in order to perform less work. This theory is controversial because it assumes that, given the chance, workers will shirk duties or slack off. It can explain behavior as obvious as not showing up for work or as subtle as performing only the tasks explicitly required, even when it is clear that they are not enough to ensure that the organization will meet its goals. In shirking, workers look after their own self-interest; they do not want to do more than they have to for their pay.

Professionalization is sometimes viewed as an antidote to these forms of self-interested behavior. Agency theory may seem more appropriate for describing entry-level workers in a fast-food restaurant than professionals in positions of responsibility. Professionalism is often thought to obviate rewards and sanctions, because standards and norms of public service bring the professional's conduct into line with the organization's and clients' interests. Critics of agency theory can argue that its premises of self-interest and conclusions of the need for rewards do not apply to such professionals as teachers.

Supporters of agency theory would respond to this objection that all people are subject to the same basic motivational psychology. Although training, education, and professional norms may lessen the need for detailed supervision and monitoring of some types of work-

---

[1]For a discussion of this theory, see Moe, Terry M., "The New Economics of Organization," *American Journal of Political Science,* Vol. 28, No. 4, 1984, pp. 739–777. The main emphasis of agency theory is not just that managers are at odds with employees who are their agents, but that managers will seek administrative strategies to help them overcome the information asymmetry inherent in the relationship. Those strategies are a common subject of analysis in agency theory.

ers, the underlying logic of employment is the same. After all, doctors, lawyers, engineers, and other professionals are rewarded with higher salaries or revenue for good performance, and are sanctioned with fewer clients and lower income for poor performance. Agency theory is believed by many to capture the basic elements of a wide range of organizational dynamics, including professional and nonprofessional employment. It is used to explain how an organization designs incentive systems and structures itself internally, how public agencies respond to congressional overseers, and even to explain why private firms exist at all.

PROFESSIONALISM

Establishing whether professionalism eliminates the need for a system of incentives is important and deserves further consideration. The argument that formal rewards and sanctions are unnecessary in a professional setting rests on the organizing principle of the professions: a worker's autonomy over his or her work. The formal components of this autonomy typically include control over recruitment and certification of workers, and establishment of standards and behavioral codes. Professions are also characterized by a socialization process for new members that produces a sense of identity and shared values. The values and internalized norms are generally explained by members of the profession in terms of an ideology of public service.[2] Professional autonomy is justified by claims to special expertise that precludes intervention and judgments by outsiders who do not have the competence to evaluate performance and allocate rewards or sanctions. Therefore, self-regulation is an important component of this system of autonomy. Professional communities offer the public an assurance of minimum standards of competence by taking responsibility for access to the profession, and for standards and accreditation.

But the presence of a system for professional standard-setting and socialization does not necessarily reduce the need for formal rewards

---

[2]See Daniels, Arlene Kaplan, "How Free Should Professionals Be?" in Eliot Friedson, ed., *The Professions and Their Prospects,* Beverly Hills, Calif.: Sage Publications, 1973, and Goode, William J., "Community Within a Community," *American Sociological Review,* Vol. 22, 1957, pp. 194–200.

and sanctions. The function of rewarding achievement—the linking of performance and salary, for instance—is not the same as ensuring that all professionals meet minimum standards of competence or share certain behavioral norms. Judgments about performance, the ranking of individuals, and the linking of rewards and career advancement to accomplishment rather than tenure are quite consistent with professionalism. The attorney who consistently wins in court, for example, is better rewarded than a colleague who loses more often than he or she wins. The higher-achieving attorney may earn more money, assume greater responsibility for major cases, and be advanced more quickly to partner status than the colleague who has the same experience and credentials and who meets the same basic standard of legal competence, but who does not perform as well.

In theory, what distinguishes the rewards and sanctions of the professional setting from those of the nonprofessional environment is that they are based on peer judgments rather than on supervisory evaluations.[3] Professionalism does not eliminate the need for controls, checks, and incentives; rather, it shifts the locus of such judgments away from managers to the members of the occupation themselves.[4] Yet while peer evaluation is an important component of professional status, in practice the degree and success of self-regulation and peer-based evaluation vary substantially among the professions.

Medicine is typically viewed as an archetype of self-regulation because of the high degree of professional autonomy granted physicians who work without direct supervision and with a prominent ideology of public service. But the structure of the client–professional relationship in medicine is quite different from that in many other professions, including teaching, so the higher degree of autonomy typical of medical self-regulation is not necessarily a good model for other professions. The traditional model of the physician who works on a fee-for-service basis in a largely private health-care

---

[3]Goode (1957).

[4]See Darling-Hammond, Linda, "Teacher Professionalism: Why and How?" in Ann Lieberman, ed., *Schools as Collaborative Cultures: Creating the Future Now,* New York: The Falmer Press, 1990.

market does not fit well the job of the school teacher, who provides a public good at taxpayer expense. Professional autonomy over work in the context of an organization such as a school should not be confused with the economic autonomy of self-employed professionals.[5] When a profession is embedded in an organization, as is generally the case for engineering and teaching, managers still control resources, although they have much less control over how workers go about performing their work.

Engineering, for example, provides little economic autonomy to workers, who are typically employed in hierarchical organizations, and who receive objectives from supervisors. The work goals of the engineer are those of the organization, and the organization provides supervision and makes judgments about performance that shape the career of the engineer.

Whether the profession of teaching is viewed as more akin to that of medicine, or engineering, or law, the claims of agency theory for the need for performance-based rewards apply. Increased professionalism in teaching is undoubtedly a good thing for schools, and the increased flexibility and discretion associated with professional work are quite consistent with decentralization. Yet many studies have found that professional self-motivation is not sufficient to ensure that people will commit themselves to a high level of performance in serving the organization's goals.[6]

This view suggests that schools should devise systems of incentives that establish meaningful connections between performance and pay or tenure. Decentralization offers a good opportunity to implement such systems, whether they rely solely on peer judgments, on evaluations by principals, or on some combination consistent with decentralized authority in the school. Establishing a successful system for rewarding performance in a decentralized organization is much easier said than done, as Chapter Five illustrates.

---

[5]See Friedson, Eliot, ed., *The Professions and Their Prospects,* Beverly Hills, Calif.: Sage Publications, 1973.

[6]See Warwick (1975) and Lipsky (1980).

RULE-FOLLOWING AND BUREAUCRACY

Efforts to provide incentives and sanctions to workers can be plagued by an unfortunate trap: Often, in turning to rules and procedures to structure employee behavior and to assess when employees are performing their jobs properly, the designers—or redesigners—of an organization are left with an incentive system that rewards employees more for compliance and strict adherence to procedures than for creativity, initiative, and results, an incentive system that is a return to the very bureaucracy that is being abandoned.

BUREAUCRACY: ITS SUCCESSES AND FAILURES

Such "bureaucratic" incentive systems need not be all bad, just as *bureaucracy* need not be a pejorative word. As organizations with codified rules and standardized procedures that specify how work is to be done, bureaucracies can be effective and efficient institutional forms for providing goods or services under certain circumstances: when there is high stability in the organization's environment, when the needs of the organization's clients are predictable, and when tasks are well understood and standardized. In such cases, the organization performs best when all its members follow procedures closely—one reason why bureaucracies are laden with red tape and why they typically reward members for compliance with rules rather than for initiative or good judgment.

McDonald's Restaurants provide a striking example of such bureaucratic success. The operation of each McDonald's franchise is specified in excruciating detail in a 600-page manual. The dimensions of french fries are specified to one thirty-second of an inch, and even the exact order in which cooks are to flip hamburgers has been centrally determined. There is little room for creativity and invention on the part of franchise employees at McDonald's. It is difficult to imagine an organization with more detailed rules and procedures.[1] Yet this organizational form is well suited to the fast-food business. It is important that the hamburgers from a McDonald's in Seattle taste like those from a store in San Diego, because much of the value of McDonald's food is that customers know what to expect, and they can rely on quick service at predictable prices. McDonald's must reward employees for their adherence to centrally determined procedures and rules.

This form of bureaucracy, which directs members' efforts toward compliance with rules, is obviously less well suited to environments in which circumstances change often, clients' needs are difficult to predict precisely, and/or the tasks being performed are not standardized. Few people doubt that schools meet these criteria. For this reason, decentralized school designs must provide incentives and sanctions for employees without falling into the trap of mandating rules specifying what is "proper" behavior or performance, such as how many hours are to be worked each day, how much time is to be spent "on task," or which lessons are to be delivered according to what schedule. There are few educational equivalents to specifying that the third row of hamburgers is to be flipped before the second row. This means that a decentralized organization must determine how to meaningfully reward performance without simply encouraging procedural compliance and rule-based assessments.

The solution lies in rethinking who has responsibility for setting goals (ends) in a school organization and who has responsibility for devising the means of fulfilling those goals. This distinction between means and ends is fundamental to the concept of decentralization, although it is rarely discussed explicitly. To see the importance of identifying responsibility for means and ends in an organization, it is worthwhile to consider the many related explanations that have been offered for what makes bureaucracies so "bureaucratic." Analyses of bureaucracy repeatedly focus on the problems associated with

---

[1]See Wilson (1989) for a description of McDonald's as a bureaucracy and for a comparison of it with other bureaucracies.

identifying responsibilities for goals and for the strategies organizations use in pursuing those goals.

There are many reasons why bureaucratic forms exist in contexts where they seem inefficient or ineffective. Perhaps the most well-accepted theory of bureaucracy says that because the specific goals of public institutions are often vague or politically contentious, organizational forms evolve in which workers tend to be evaluated on how well they follow rules rather than on how much they contribute to performance and the achievement of goals.[2] The employees running a national park provide a good example of this problem.

The formal goal, or mission, of the National Park Service is to administer and preserve land for the benefit and enjoyment of U.S. citizens. At this level of abstraction, that goal is not especially open to contention. But in practice, this simple mission collapses into often-conflicting goals. The park may want to set up hotels, buses, and conveniences so that the greatest number of people can visit the park, including those who are physically disabled and may require special technology. On the other hand, the park may want to limit access to a smaller number of people so that there is less impact on the ecosystem, requiring visitors to walk and stay in primitive facilities. Further conflicts are whether the park ranger should turn away a busload of visitors who have arrived just at closing time, reducing overnight human impact, or should open the gates to allow more people to enjoy the park; and whether extra people in a large party should be allowed to occupy a small campsite. These are conflicts between a preservationist interpretation of the organization's goals and a recreational one.

The decisions that a Park Service employee makes about how to enforce various rules or about what tactics to take in managing park visitation have implications that are the subject of a current national political debate over the mission of U.S. parks. In the face of public controversy, park rangers and their supervisors may find it best to simply follow written rules assiduously. By adhering closely to rules, formal procedures, and "red tape," the local park employee can pass

---

[2]Wilson (1989) and Warwick (1975).

along responsibility for conflicting policy decisions to supervisors and managers. By exercising little personal discretion, and by adhering to formal procedures for opening and closing times, park capacity, and visitor conveniences, the ranger cannot be blamed by either side in the controversy over Park Service stewardship of federal lands. A ranger might appear inflexible and bureaucratic, but will not be dragged into controversy. After all, the ranger who allows extra park usage may be criticized by environmentalists for harming the land, and the ranger who cuts back on conveniences and hours may be denounced by the local chamber of commerce for making the park less hospitable to out-of-town visitors. In short, there may be circumstances in which the ranger is rewarded for acting like a "bureaucrat."

But bureaucratic behavior is not always the result of conflicting goals. Another explanation for why organizations become so obsessed with bureaucratic rule-following is that employees can become overwhelmed with the difficulty of handling clients' problems, especially when resources are limited. In such a case, it may simply be impossible to achieve formal goals, however clear and unambiguous they are. Employees charged with an impossible mission may assume a defensive posture, falling back on adherence to rules to prove that they are doing their job.[3] An example might be the caseworker at a county welfare department, where the goal of the office is to provide comprehensive social services to a large population of poverty-stricken citizens. Budget restrictions mean that there is not enough money to go around, and there are far too few employees to administer the caseload. Actually assisting everyone who requests help is out of the question.

The result of this situation is the caseworker who insists that forms be filled out precisely, disqualifies a client for an obviously needed service on a technicality, moves lethargically despite a long line waiting for service, and departs promptly at 5:00 p.m. every day. Given the agency's difficult circumstances, this worker may choose to follow rules as closely as possible, rather than face the frustration

---

[3]See Nordlinger, Eric, *Decentralizing the City: A Study of Boston's Little City Halls*, Cambridge, Mass.: MIT Press, 1972.

and lack of reward that would come from trying to achieve impossible goals.

One classic theory of organization refers to these phenomena as "goal displacements," meaning that rules and procedures that are devised as means to the organization's end eventually develop into an end in themselves.[4] Workers begin to see rule-following as their primary goal, rather than as a way to achieve a higher objective.

Such bureaucratic rule-following may, in fact, be a logical, or rational, response to the work situation. Some scholars have used the terms "functional rationality" and "substantial rationality" to describe this tension between rule-following and working to benefit the client.[5] When workers strive to carry out procedures and adhere closely to rules, they are exercising functional rationality: They use their judgment and skills to adhere to the rules to perform a well-defined function. This is *rational* because it is the behavior for which they are best rewarded. On the other hand, when workers use their judgment and skills to devise solutions to client problems on their own, when they judge for themselves what would be best in a given situation, they are exercising *substantial* rationality: Rather than follow rules, they make substantive decisions about their work.

The point of this distinction is that functional and substantial rationality do not arise because of personality traits or individuals' temperaments, but from the system of rewards and sanctions that structures the work environment.   Centralized, rule-oriented bureaucracies are often associated with functional rationality, because they tend to reward workers for rule-following. Decentralized organizations are often associated with substantial rationality, because they give flexibility to local units and reward workers for solving problems.

Another school of thought on organizations observes that a focus on rules rather than results is often the effect of the environmental con-

---

[4]See Merton, Robert K., *Social Theory and Social Structure*, Glencoe, Ill.: The Free Press, 1957.

[5]This theory is Mannheim's. For a discussion, see Meyer, Marshall W., *Bureaucratic Structure and Authority: Coordination and Control in 254 Government Agencies*, New York: Harper and Row, 1972.

straints placed on an organization. In this view, certain classes of organizations are "adaptive" rather than productive:[6] They organize themselves and expend energy toward adapting to their political or economic environment rather than toward efficiently producing an output or service.[7] Whereas private firms organize themselves to be productive in the marketplace, adaptive organizations do not structure themselves in the same way, because they have no "product" to sell. They operate on different goals, focusing on responding to political demands, meeting regulations, keeping constituents happy, and meeting commitments of a nonmarket nature, because these are what is required for the organization to survive.

These theories about the nature of bureaucracy point to the importance of connections between individuals' incentives and the organization's approach to means and ends. The success of decentralization and the elimination of unwanted bureaucracy lie in large measure in finding ways to separate responsibility for establishing goals from responsibility for setting up the means for achieving those goals.

DIVIDING RESPONSIBILITY FOR MEANS AND ENDS: THE "CONTRACT"

Successfully decentralized organizations are generally designed with central authorities that tell local units what is to be done, in general terms, but that do not tell them how to do it. Higher authorities decide on goals and specify desired outcomes but leave local units to decide on the means used to achieve those goals. In the process, the local units are given sufficient control over resources to exercise discretion. In his review of dozens of bureaucracies, Wilson found almost universally that those which were effectively decentralized

---

[6]A number of organizations, or subunits within larger organizations, demonstrate this characteristic. Service and professional organizations most commonly fit this description, including hospitals, the YMCA, and religious organizations. For a review, see Scott, W. Richard, *Organizations: Rational, Natural, and Open Systems*, 3rd ed., New York: Prentice-Hall, 1992.

[7]Meyer, John W., W. Richard Scott, and Terrence E. Deal, "Institutional and Technical Sources of Organizational Structure: Explaining the Structure of Educational Organizations," in Herman D. Stein, ed., *Organization and the Human Services: Cross-Disciplinary Reflections*, Philadelphia: Temple University Press, 1981, p. 165.

demonstrated this characteristic.[8] For decentralization to succeed, central authorities must be prepared to accept a division of labor between goal specification and selection of means. They must permit local units to decide for themselves how to go about their jobs.

One of the main problems with centralized bureaucracies is that they choose goals and specify means, assigning the local unit responsibility only for adhering to those goals—for following rules. In a centralized system, people in local units are employed to perform tasks or routines specified from above, whereas in a truly decentralized system, people are employed to achieve results. The central authority still monitors performance but does not prescribe methods and procedures.[9]

A division of labor over decisions about means and ends can be thought of as a contract that specifies goals and is agreed to, by the central authority and the local unit, at a specified price. The contract sets a level of performance but does not specify the methods or the allocation of resources to be used. It permits the central authority to determine and convey goals for the delivery of a service, and it provides the contractor with discretion over what means to choose in achieving those goals. The contract does not specify how the contractor, the local unit, is to organize itself, whom it is to employ, nor what methods it will choose, except within a minimum of constraints and guidelines. The local unit is judged periodically on whether it is achieving those goals and is held accountable only for fulfilling the terms of its agreement.[10]

In such a contract, the discretion gained by the local unit comes with new obligations. The local unit cannot escape responsibility for poor

---

[8]Wilson (1989).

[9]Hill, Paul T., and Josephine J. Bonan, *Decentralization and Accountability in Public Education*, Santa Monica, Calif.: RAND, R-4066-MCF/IET, 1991.

[10]See Wilson (1989) on the distinction between rule-based and contractual systems of administration. Note that decentralization and local control under a "contract" model do not mean a complete absence of political regulation or administrative oversight. A decentralized school, like other decentralized organizations, may be expected to meet certain requirements for fairness, nondiscrimination and safety—requirements that are intended to prevent the abuse of certain basic rights that we expect students to be afforded but that do not extend beyond protection to the specification of educational methods and means.

performance by claiming that it has followed proper procedures.[11] On the contrary, a decentralized system requires that the local unit take responsibility for initiating its own self-assessment. In order to fulfill its part of the bargain, the local unit needs information about its own performance, because *accountability* is not defined in terms of compliance with rules but in terms of an obligation to fulfill the goals of the contract.

As a governance instrument, a contract allows the central authority to determine and convey goals for the delivery of a service, and it provides the contractor with discretion over what means to choose for achieving the goals. As a conceptual model for a decentralized organization, a contract is the opposite of a rule-based approach to public administration. Most public schools—even most of those claiming to be decentralized—are classic cases of organizations that reward rule-following rather than results. Schools are designed as much around compliance with rules set by the state and district as around meeting educational goals. In the U.S. "schools succeed or fail according to their conformity to institutional rules, rather than by the effectiveness of their technical performance."[12]

A contract-inspired form of decentralization entails a great deal more than setting up advisory panels or local decisionmaking committees that help select teachers or textbooks within the existing adminstrative framework. Dividing responsibility for decisions about means and ends suggests the need for a radically new relationship between schools and main offices, in which schools have discretion over the major decisions affecting their structure and operations. Districts, on the other hand, would have primary discretion over the setting of goals and standards, although these may be the result of negotiation and discussion.

This contract-inspired relationship may take a form similar to that between district offices and "grant-maintained" schools in Great Britain. The 1988 Education Reform Act in Britain enabled schools to "opt-out" of the administration of the local education authorities (LEAs) that run the nation's schools. After voting to opt-out, schools

---

[11]Wilson (1989).

[12]Meyer, Scott, and Deal (1981), p. 165.

acquire what is known as grant-maintained status, which means that they are not only freed of administrative control by the LEAs but that they receive an increased budget equivalent to their share of administrative costs previously spent at the LEA. The schools have authority over a range of decisions that would otherwise be controlled by administrators at the LEAs.[13] Such schools operate, in a sense, by contract, because they agree to meet centrally determined educational goals but are free to organize themselves and make decisions about how to carry out their goals as they see fit.

---

[13]Chubb, John E., and Terry M. Moe, *A Lesson in School Reform from Great Britain*, Washington, D.C.: The Brookings Institution, 1992.

Chapter Six

DECENTRALIZATION IN SCHOOLS

From the theories of bureaucracy reviewed above, I have extracted several principles for guiding school decentralization. The principles can be summarized as follows:

- Successful decentralization comes from giving real increases in decisionmaking authority to those closest to the work itself; central administrators must be prepared to lose discretion over the full range of governance decisions.

- Decentralized management systems for schools should be guided by goals that distinguish between the need for better representation on the one hand, which may call for forms of group decisionmaking, and, on the other hand, the need for more administrative autonomy from main offices, which calls for strong leadership by principals.

- Decentralized organizations should establish incentive systems that reward the performance of employees.

- Decentralization can be thought of as a contract between district and school that divides responsibility for ends and means and diminishes the importance of compliance and rule-following.

The experiences that most school districts in the U.S. have had so far with decentralization reflect few of these principles. School decentralization is often marginalized and incomplete, and seeks to achieve conflicting goals. In terms of what may be the most important of the principles, the contract between district and school, the results, almost invariably, look less like a wholly restructured contract between school and district than like the old centralized system that was meant to be replaced.

A good example of such shortcomings is provided by site-based management (SBM), the most common incarnation of school decentralization. SBM is too often viewed as a scheme that can be added to a menu of other reforms, rather than as a fundamental change in how decisions—all decisions—are made in a school system. Many schools claim to employ site-based management. In 1990, seven of the eight largest school districts in the United States claimed to be using SBM. But in most, very little decisionmaking was really decentralized.[1] Site-based management is commonly applied to only a small subset of the constellation of decisions that go into running a school system. Some districts have decentralized decisions about part of their budgets but not about personnel or curriculum; some have decentralized aspects of curriculum only; and others have decentralized a different combination. Often, SBM plans give authority to schools over only marginal issues: for example, safety, career education, and parent involvement. SBM generally does little to change the fact that most schools have discretion over much less than 10 percent of the money spent within their walls.

There are several reasons why delegations of authority can turn out to be illusory. District offices sometimes retain the authority to approve or disapprove decisions made at the school, or they constrain schools' authority by limiting the range of decisions that can be made.[2] Districts sometimes maintain responsibility for implementing decisions made at the school, keeping de facto control. In practice, decentralization plans too often suffer from disagreement over whether decentralization is primarily intended to draw more people—teachers and parents—into the decisionmaking process or whether it is primarily intended to make schools more autonomous

---

[1]Malen B., R. Ogawa, and J. Kranz, "What Do We Know About School-Based Management? A Case Study of the Literature—A Call For Research," in W. H. Cluen and J. F. Witte, eds., *Choice and Control in American Education*, Vol. 23, Philadelphia: Falmer Press, 1990, cited in Wohlstetter, Priscilla, and Allan Odden, *Rethinking School-Based Management Policy and Research*, Los Angeles: University of Southern California, Center for Research in Education Finance, Working Paper No. 11, January 1992.

[2]Wohlstetter and Odden (1992).

from central-office bureaucracies. Because of this disagreement, and because of the reluctance of boards, superintendents, and other administrators to relinquish real power, decentralization plans often result in fragmented decisionmaking authority, adding even more complexity to administrative processes.

The well-known New York City School Decentralization Act of 1969 is a vivid example of how decentralization efforts can divide and complicate school administration, because it split decisionmaking authority among many levels of hierarchy, including the new Community School Boards created in the name of local control. In its first two years, the plan precipitated thirty-one major lawsuits over the distribution of power. That attempt at decentralization, like many, resulted in a complex, hybrid form of administration in which internal tensions are rampant.[3]

The lackluster success that so many school decentralization efforts have enjoyed highlights the need for a well-defined vision of what decentralization means, and a more comprehensive restructuring of decisionmaking authority, incentive systems, and relationships between schools and district offices.

---

[3]See LaNoue, George R., and Bruce R. Smith, *The Politics of School Decentralization*, Lexington, Mass.: Lexington Books, 1973, and Gittell, Marilyn, *School Boards and School Policy: An Evaluation of Decentralization in New York City*, New York: Praeger Publishers, 1973.

BIBLIOGRAPHY

Astley, W. Graham, and Andrew H. Van de Ven, "Central Perspectives and Debates in Organization Theory," *Administrative Science Quarterly*, Vol. 28, 1983, pp. 245–273.

Bidwell, Charles E., "The School as a Formal Organization," in Yeheskel Hasenfeld and Richard A. English, eds., *Human Service Organizations*, Ann Arbor.: The University of Michigan Press, 1974.

Blau, Peter M., and W. Richard Scott, *Formal Organizations: A Comparative Approach*, San Francisco: Chandler Publishing Company, 1962.

Chubb, John E., and Terry M. Moe, *A Lesson in School Reform from Great Britain*, Washington, D.C.: The Brookings Institution, 1992.

Cillie, Francois S., *Centralization or Decentralization: A Study in Educational Adaptation*, New York: Columbia University, Teachers College Bureau of Publications, 1940.

Coleman, James S., et al., *Equality of Educational Opportunity*, Washington, D.C.: U.S. Department of Education, 1966.

Corwin, Ronald G., "The Formulation of Goals in the Public Schools," in Yeheskel Hasenfeld and Richard A. English, eds., *Human Service Organizations*, Ann Arbor: The University of Michigan Press, 1974.

Daniels, Arlene Kaplan, "How Free Should Professionals Be?" in Eliot Friedson, ed., *The Professions and Their Prospects*, Beverly Hills, Calif.: Sage Publications, 1973.

Darling-Hammond, Linda, "Teacher Professionalism: Why and How?" in Ann Lieberman, ed., *Schools as Collaborative Cultures: Creating the Future Now*, New York: The Falmer Press, 1990.

Doyle, Denis P., and Chester E. Finn, Jr., "American Schools and the Future of Local Control," *The Public Interest*, No. 77, Fall 1984, pp. 77–95.

Fantini, Mario, "Participation, Decentralization, Community Control and Quality Education," *Teachers College Record*, Vol. 71, September 1969, pp. 93–107.

Fantini, Mario, and Marilyn Gittell, *Community Control and the Urban School*, New York: Praeger Publishers, 1971.

Fein, Leonard, *The Ecology of the Public Schools: An Inquiry into Community Control*, New York: Pegasus, 1971.

Friedson, Eliot, ed., *The Professions and Their Prospects*, Beverly Hills, Calif.: Sage Publications, 1973.

Gittell, Marilyn, *School Boards and Public Policy: An Evaluation of Decentralization in New York City*, New York: Praeger Publishers, 1973.

Goode, William J., "Community Within a Community," *American Sociological Review*, Vol. 22, 1957, pp. 194–200.

Hasenfeld, Yeheskel, and Richard A. English, eds., *Human Service Organizations*, Ann Arbor: The University of Michigan Press, 1974.

Hill, Paul T., and Josephine J. Bonan, *Decentralization and Accountability in Public Education*, Santa Monica, Calif.: RAND, R-4066-MCF/IET, 1991.

Kaufman, Herbert, *The Limits of Organizational Change*, University: University of Alabama Press, 1971.

Kristol, Irving, "Decentralization for What?" *The Public Interest*, No. 11, Spring 1968, pp. 17–25.

LaNoue, George R., and Bruce R. Smith, *The Politics of School Decentralization*, Lexington, Mass.: Lexington Books, 1973.

Lipsky, Michael, *Street-Level Bureaucracy*, New York: Russell Sage Foundation, 1980.

Lopate, Carol, Erwin Flaxman, Effie M. Bynum, and Edmund W. Gordon, "Decentralization and Community Participation in Public Education," *Review of Educational Research*, Vol. 40, No. 1, February 1970, pp. 135–150.

March, James, and Herbert Simon, *Organizations*, New York: Wiley, 1958.

Merton, Robert K., "Bureaucratic Structure and Personality," *Social Forces*, Vol. 17, May 1970, pp. 560–568.

——, *Social Theory and Social Structure*, Glencoe, Ill.: The Free Press, 1957.

Meyer, John W., W. Richard Scott, and Terrence E. Deal, "Institutional and Technical Sources of Organizational Structure: Explaining the Structure of Educational Organizations," in Herman D. Stein, ed., *Organization and the Human Services: Cross-Disciplinary Reflections*, Philadelphia: Temple University Press, 1981.

Meyer, John W., W. Richard Scott, and David Strang, "Centralization, Fragmentation, and School District Complexity," *Administrative Science Quarterly*, Vol. 32, 1987, pp. 186–201.

Meyer, Marshall W., *Bureaucratic Structure and Authority: Coordination and Control in 254 Government Agencies*, New York: Harper and Row, 1972.

Moe, Terry M., "The New Economics of Organization," *American Journal of Political Science*, Vol. 28, No.4, 1984, pp. 739–777.

Mort, Paul R., and Francis G. Cornell, *American Schools in Transition: How Our Schools Adapt Their Practices to Changing Needs*, New York: Teachers College Press, 1941.

Mosher, Frederick C., *Governmental Reorganizations*, New York: Bobbs-Merrill Company, 1967.

Nordlinger, Eric A., *Decentralizing the City: A Study of Boston's Little City Halls*, Cambridge, Mass.: MIT Press, 1972.

Odden, Allan, and Sharon Conley, *Restructuring Teacher Compensation Systems to Foster Collegiallity and Help Accomplish National Education Goals*, Los Angeles: University of Southern California, Center for Research in Education Finance, Working Paper No. 2, September 1991.

Odden, Allan, and Lori Kim, *National Goals and Interstate Disparities: A New Federal Role in School Finance*, Los Angeles: University of Southern California, Center for Research in Education Finance, Working Paper No. 8, September 1991.

Odden, Allan, and Nancy Kotowski, *A New School Finance for Public School Choice*, Los Angeles: University of Southern California, Center for Research in Education Finance, Working Paper No. 3, September 1991.

Ornstein, Allan C., "Decentralizing Urban Schools," *Journal of Secondary Education*, Vol. 46, No. 2, February 1971, pp. 83–91.

Osborne, David, and Ted Gaebler, *Reinventing Government: How the Entrepreneurial Spirit Is Transforming the Public Sector*, New York: Addison-Wesley, 1992.

Perrow, Charles, "The Analysis of Goals in Complex Organizations," in Yeheskel Hasenfeld and Richard A. English, eds., *Human Service Organizations*, Ann Arbor: The University of Michigan Press, 1974.

Purkey, S. C., and M. S. Smith, "Effective Schools: A Review," *Elementary School Journal*, Vol. 83, 1983, pp. 426–452.

Scott, W. Richard, *Organizations: Rational, Natural, and Open Systems*, 3rd ed., New York: Prentice-Hall, 1992.

Selznick, Philip, "An Approach to the Theory of Organization," *American Sociological Review*, Vol. 8, No. 1, February 1948, pp. 47–54.

——, *TVA and the Grass Roots: A Study of Politics and Organization*, Berkeley: University of California Press, 1949.

Stedman, Lawrence C., "A New Look at the Effective Schools Literature," *Urban Education*, Vol. 20, 1985, pp. 295–326.

Strang, David, "The Administrative Transformation of American Education: School District Consolidation, 1938–1980," *Administrative Science Quarterly*, Vol. 32, 1987, pp. 352–366.

Warwick, Donald P., *A Theory of Public Bureaucracy: Politics, Personality, and Organization in the State Department*, Cambridge, Mass.: Harvard University, 1975.

Weber, Max, *From Max Weber: Essays in Sociology*, Hans H. Gerth and C. Wright Mills, eds., Oxford: Oxford University Press, 1946.

———, *The Theory of Social and Economic Organization*, Talcott Parsons, ed., New York: The Free Press, 1957.

Wilson, James Q., *Bureaucracy: What Government Agencies Do and Why They Do It*, New York: Basic Books, 1989.

Wohlstetter, Priscilla, and Allan Odden, *Rethinking School-Based Management Policy and Research*, Los Angeles: University of Southern California, Center for Research in Education Finance, Working Paper No. 11, January 1992.

Yin, Robert K., and Douglas Yates, *Street-Level Governments*, Lexington, Mass.: Lexington Books, 1975.